Land of Legend

Tennessee is a state of legendary natural beauty and inspiring folk culture. The mountains and valleys of the state have supported human communities for more than ten thousand years. The climate is mild, the soil is rich, and the woodlands are thick with wildlife. The first Europeans to settle the area were trappers, trading with Native Americans for furs and living in the wild. They were followed by farmers from North Carolina and Virginia, who crossed the mountains in search of fertile land. The land they found would influence the character of the state for years to come. East Tennessee's terrain was hilly, best suited to small farms. The men and women who settled there had an independent, hard-working, self-reliant spirit that led them to back the antislavery Union when the Civil War began. The more fertile soil of Middle and West Tennessee was ideal for large-scale farming operations, dependent on slave labor. Cotton and tobacco were mainstays of the regions' economies. As a result, those parts of the state sided with the Confederacy. The political and economic divisions were apparent well into the twentieth century.

From its early pioneers, the legendary volunteer spirit of Tennessee grew. Scouts and explorers, such as Davy Crockett, came to represent the heroic individualism of Tennesseeans. Tennessee heroes had a deep connection to the land, as well as a spirit of adventure. Tennessee has continued to nurture free spirits who still have a strong link to home. Tennessee writers James Agee and Nikki Giovanni are famous for their sensitive portrayals of the human condition, while the unique sounds of Tennessee musicians such as Elvis Presley have blended the traditions of mountain music with the newer rhythms of rock and roll. The riches of the Tennessee spirit are mirrored in the riches of the land, which create a diverse economy that protects and celebrates the old while nurturing the new. Tennessee is a land where legends will always be made.

▶ Map of Tennessee showing the interstate highway system, as well as major cities and waterways.

▼ Pioneer Farmstead in Great Smoky Mountains National Park.

TENNESSEE

KENTUCKY — *L. Barkley*
VIRGINIA

MISSOURI

ARK.

Clarksville

Nashville

Kentucky L.

Spring Hill

Smyrna

Cumberland R.

Oak Ridge

Kingsport

Johnson City

Center Hill L.

Knoxville

Tennessee R.

Murfreesboro

Watts Bar L.

Gatlinburg

NORTH CAROLINA

Jackson

Dayton

Mississippi R.

Memphis

Chattanooga

MISSISSIPPI   **ALABAMA**   Huntsville   **GEORGIA**

N

SCALE/KEY

0	100 Miles
0	100 Kilometers

⭐ Capital

– ·· – State Border

🛡 Interstate Highways

Fast Facts

TENNESSEE (TN), The Volunteer State

Entered Union

June 1, 1796 (16th state)

Capital	Population
Nashville	569,891

Total Population (2000)

5,689,283 (16th most populous state) — *Between 1990 and 2000, population of Tennessee increased 16.7 percent.*

Largest Cities

Memphis	650,100
Nashville	569,891
Knoxville	173,890
Chattanooga	155,554
Clarksville	103,455

Land Area

41,217 square miles (106,752 square kilometers) (34th largest state)

State Motto

"Agriculture and Commerce"

State Songs

"My Homeland, Tennessee," *by Nell Grayson Taylor and Roy Lamont Smith, adopted in 1925;* "When It's Iris Time in Tennessee," *by Willa Waid Newman, adopted in 1935;* "The Tennessee Waltz," *by Pee Wee King and Redd Stewart, adopted in 1965;* "Rocky Top," *by Boudleaux and Felice Bryan, adopted in 1982;* "Tennessee," *by Vivian Rorie, adopted in 1992; and* "The Pride of Tennessee," *by Fred Congdon, Thomas Vaughn, and Carol Elliot, adopted in 1996.*

State Animal

Raccoon

State Bird

Mockingbird — *One of the finest singers among North American birds, it is known for its ability to mimic the songs of other birds, as well as sing its own beautiful song.*

State Game Fish

Largemouth bass — *This fish can grow to more than 10 pounds (4.5 kilograms) and is known for its fighting ability.*

State Insects

Firefly and lady beetle (ladybug) — *The ladybug is often used to control insect pests because it feeds on insects and their eggs.*

State Tree

Tulip poplar — *Pioneers used the tulip poplar to build houses and other buildings.*

State Flower

Iris — *There are many species of iris and a variety of colors. When the state legislature chose the iris as the state flower, it never specified the color, but most Tennesseeans consider purple to be the official color.*

State Horse

Tennessee walking horse

PLACES TO VISIT

Lost Sea, *Sweetwater*
The United States's largest underground lake, a registered national landmark, features a guided walk through rooms as well as a ride on large, glass-bottom boats.

Country Music Hall of Fame and Museum, *Nashville*
This brand-new facility offers live music, three theaters, and a wide variety of interactive exhibits. Songwriters and other musicians, costume designers, and dance instructors share their techniques as part of the tour experience.

Cumberland Gap National Historical Park, *Cumberland Gap*
Journey back into history, trace the footsteps of Daniel Boone, and discover spectacular views and incredible scenery. Located where the borders of Tennessee, Kentucky, and Virginia meet.

For other places and events, see p. 44.

BIGGEST, BEST, AND MOST

- Tennessee is known as the hardwood flooring capital of the United States.
- The *Grand Ole Opry* is the longest-running live radio program in the world. It has been broadcast every Saturday night since 1925.

STATE FIRSTS

- **1772** The first written constitution in what is now the United States was drafted by the Wautauga Association, a group of early Tennessee settlers, at Sycamore Shoals near Elizabethton.
- **1866** Tennessee became the first former Confederate state to be readmitted to the Union after the Civil War's end.
- **1905** Nashville became home to America's first African-American architectural firm, McKissack and McKissack.

Fine Feathers

The lavish Peabody Hotel in Memphis has some unusual residents — ducks. There have been ducks at the Peabody since the 1930s, when a hotel manager placed live ducks in the lobby fountain, initially as a joke. They became popular with hotel guests and are now a beloved fixture in Memphis. The ducks (mallards) live in a special room in the penthouse of the hotel. Every morning, they march down to the fountain to musical accompaniment, and they return to their room in the late afternoon.

Sweet Originals

Tennessee is known for salty country ham, fluffy biscuits, grits, and red-eye gravy, as well as two confections with unusual names — GooGoos and MoonPies. The GooGoo Cluster, made by the Standard Candy Company in Nashville, has been around since 1912 and is claimed to be the nation's first "combination" candy bar. It's available in several flavors today, but the original version contains marshmallow, caramel, and peanuts, all covered in milk chocolate. It gets its name from the claim that it is so delicious that "people will ask for it from birth." The MoonPie comes from Chattanooga and has been around since 1917. It consists of a layer of marshmallow sandwiched between two cookies and dipped in a chocolate, vanilla, or banana coating.

In 1775, Henderson's Transylvania Company purchased more than 20 million acres (8 million hectares) of Tennessee land from the Cherokee. Many Cherokee leaders opposed the sale, and as more and more settlers arrived, relations between the two groups began to sour.

Not long after the Transylvania Purchase, thirteen of Britain's North American colonies began to fight for their independence in the Revolutionary War (1775–1783). Tennessee saw little fighting, but many Tennesseeans fought for the cause of independence. In 1780, Tennessee volunteers known as the "Overmountain Men" helped defeat British and Loyalist (pro-British colonist) forces at the Battle of Kings Mountain, South Carolina. At about the same time, settlers built Fort Nashborough, which was renamed Nashville in 1784, along the Cumberland River.

After the war, North Carolina claimed Tennessee as the Washington District. By this time, fighting had broken out between settlers and the Native American tribes in the region, but the government of North Carolina could do little to protect the faraway settlements. In 1784, delegates met to form a new, separate state that they called Frankland, or "the land of the free," with John Sevier as governor. This new "state" was soon renamed Franklin, after the great scientist and statesman Benjamin Franklin. However, neither North Carolina nor the U.S. Congress recognized Franklin as a state, and it became part of North Carolina again in 1788.

Statehood

In 1789, North Carolina gave control of Tennessee to the federal government. The following year, William Blount became governor of the region, now called the Territory of the United States South of the River Ohio. The territory's population grew quickly, and, in 1796, with a population of some eighty thousand, Tennessee's petition for statehood was accepted. Tennessee was admitted as the sixteenth state in the Union on June 1, 1796. John Sevier became Tennessee's first

▲ Andrew Jackson of Tennessee was the hero of the Battle of New Orleans in the War of 1812.

Frontier Fighter

Born in Limestown, Davy Crockett (1786–1836) was the most famous frontier scout and hunter of his day. Also known for his wit and storytelling skills, Crockett served in the U.S. House of Representatives from 1827 to 1831 and again from 1833 to 1835. Although it was not popular to do so at the time, he was a defender of the rights of Native Americans. This stance led to his defeat in his next bid for Congress, after which he left Tennessee for Texas. Crockett died at the Alamo, fighting for Texas's independence from Mexico.

governor, and Knoxville its first capital. The capital moved to Nashville, back to Knoxville, then to Murfreesboro, and back again to Nashville before the state legislature officially named Nashville as the capital in 1843.

In 1812, the United States again went to war with Britain. That conflict, the War of 1812 (1812–1815), saw Tennesseean Andrew Jackson's rise to national fame as a soldier. Jackson achieved the rank of general and won several important victories over the British and their Native American allies. Settlers flooded into Tennessee at the war's end, and their ever-increasing hunger for land opened the saddest chapter in the history of Tennessee's Native Americans.

In 1818, the United States bought land in western Tennessee. Memphis, now Tennessee's largest city, was founded a year later on former Chickasaw land. In 1830, Congress passed the Indian Removal Act, which would force Native Americans in Tennessee, Georgia, Alabama, and other states to leave their homelands and move west to Indian Territory (now Oklahoma). The U.S. Supreme Court declared the act unconstitutional, but the act had the support of Andrew Jackson, who was now president. In 1835, the Cherokee signed a treaty surrendering their land in Tennessee, and they were led on a forced march of about 1,000 miles (1,609 km) west to Oklahoma. Many died along the way, and the march became known as the "Trail of Tears." By the end of the 1830s, only about one thousand Cherokee remained in Tennessee.

Divided Nation, Divided State

Tennessee's geography had much to do with how its citizens felt about slavery. Rugged, hilly East Tennessee was home mainly to small farmers, few of whom owned slaves. Middle Tennessee and West Tennessee, however, depended heavily on crops worked by slaves and the commerce those crops supported.

The Cherokee Alphabet

Sequoyah (c.1770–1843) was born in the mountains of eastern Tennessee to a Cherokee mother and an English father. He was known as Sequoyah to his Cherokee family but was also given the name George Gist. He never attended school, but while working as a silversmith, Sequoyah became interested in the written language used by European settlers and decided to create an alphabet for his own people. He started work on it in 1809 and finished it twelve years later. Sequoyah's eighty-five-letter alphabet was actually a syllabary — a writing system in which each letter stood for a syllable in the spoken Cherokee language. After teaching the system to his daughter, Ayoka, Sequoyah demonstrated its usefulness to a council of elders. The system proved easy to learn and was successfully used by the Cherokee people. Before long, a Cherokee-language newspaper, the *Cherokee Phoenix*, began publication. Sequoyah moved west in 1829 to present-day Oklahoma. He died in what is now Texas.

state's population. The Census of 1900 found that Tennessee was now home to more than two million people.

The early decades of the twentieth century were a time of social change and new ideas. Much of Tennessee, however, remained rural, conservative, and uncomfortable with ideas that many felt clashed with religion and tradition. The most famous example of this clash was the 1925 Scopes "Monkey Trial," in which John T. Scopes, a Dayton teacher, was tried for teaching Darwin's theory of evolution.

The Great Depression

In 1929, the New York stock market crashed, and over the next few years the nation's economy slid into a devastating depression. The South was hit especially hard.

In 1933, Franklin Delano Roosevelt took office as president, promising the nation a "New Deal." Roosevelt began a number of government programs aimed at easing some of the suffering caused by the Great Depression.

Among the most ambitious of these New Deal programs was the Tennessee Valley Authority (TVA). By constructing a series of dams along the Tennessee River, the TVA provided cheap hydroelectric power to the region's people, many of whom had never had electricity before. The TVA also tamed

The Scopes Trial

In 1925, a famous court case took place in Tennessee. A Tennessee legislator had introduced a bill banning the teaching of the theory of evolution in public schools. He believed that students should learn only the biblical story of creation. The bill became law, and a high school biology teacher, John Scopes, was arrested in Dayton for teaching evolution. A trial followed, with former presidential candidate William Jennings Bryan representing the state and celebrated attorney Clarence Darrow representing Scopes. While Scopes was found guilty of breaking the law, the Supreme Court of Tennessee eventually reversed the judgement based on a legal error.

the river's frequent floods and built sewage treatment facilities.

The Postwar Years

For Tennessee, as for the rest of the South, the major event in the decades after World War II was the rise of the Civil Rights Movement. For close to a century, most southern African Americans had been forced to live as second-class citizens in their own country. Most could not vote, and southern society was based upon segregation — separation of the races.

By the mid-1950s, African Americans were demanding the guarantee of civil rights and an end to segregation. Slowly, the South began to change. African Americans began to take their rightful place at the voting booth and in society. In Tennessee, the slow process of integrating public schools began in 1956. In 1964, A. W. Willis, Jr., became the first African American elected to the Tennessee legislature. A year later, Benjamin Hooks, a close associate of the great civil rights leader Martin Luther King, Jr., was named the first African-American criminal court judge in the state's history.

Although integration was achieved more peacefully in Tennessee than in some other southern states, Memphis witnessed a great tragedy on April 4, 1968, when Martin Luther King, Jr., was murdered outside a motel in the city.

Today's Tennessee

Another major postwar development in the state was the rise of tourism. Country-music fans flocked to Nashville — often called "Music City." Others traveled to the Great Smoky Mountains National Park, founded in 1934. The year 1982 saw two events bring even more visitors to the state — the World's Fair, held at Knoxville, and the opening of Graceland, Elvis Presley's Memphis mansion.

Tennessee, once the land of cotton and corn, became a major center of automobile manufacturing in the last decades of the twentieth century. The Japanese car manufacturer Nissan built a plant near Smyrna in 1982, and General Motors opened a factory at Spring Hill to make its line of Saturn cars in 1990.

Manhattan Project

During World War II, signs like the one above were commonplace in Oak Ridge, Tennessee. In 1942 this small town near Knoxville became home to a monumental government project. Oak Ridge was transformed almost overnight into a major scientific and industrial center as part of the "Manhattan Project" — the United States's successful, top-secret program to develop an atomic bomb. The results of this project made possible the dropping of two atomic bombs on Japan in August 1945, which resulted in Japan's surrender and the end of the war.

Tennessee Volunteers

> Now I know we had no money
> But I was rich as I could be
> In my coat of many colors
> My mamma made for me
>
> — *Dolly Parton, from "Coat of Many Colors," 1971*

Present-day Tennesseeans are largely descended from settlers who arrived in the eighteenth and nineteenth centuries. These settlers were mostly English, Scots-Irish (people of Scottish ancestry who lived in Ireland, which was then ruled by Britain), Huguenot (French Protestants), and German. With a population today that is about 80 percent white and slightly over 16 percent African American, the state has a relatively small percentage of residents who are from other ethnic backgrounds. Native Americans, for example, make up only 0.3 percent of the population. The number of people living in Tennessee who were born in the state is higher than the national average. There has been relatively little immigration to Tennessee from countries outside the United States.

Age Distribution in Tennessee (2000 Census)	
0–4	374,880
5–19	1,186,152
20–24	386,345
25–44	1,718,428
45–64	1,320,167
65 & over	703,311

Patterns of Immigration

The total number of people who immigrated to Tennessee in 1999 was 2,548. Of that number, the largest immigrant groups were from Mexico (12%), India (8%), and China (5%).

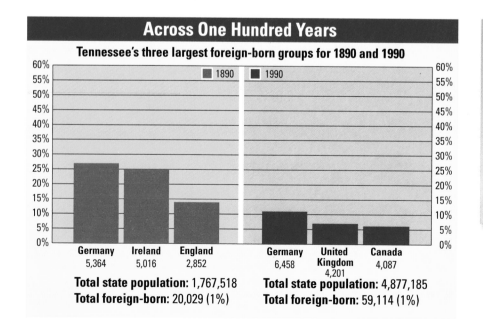

Across One Hundred Years

Tennessee's three largest foreign-born groups for 1890 and 1990

Legend: 1890, 1990

	Germany 5,364	Ireland 5,016	England 2,852

Total state population: 1,767,518
Total foreign-born: 20,029 (1%)

	Germany 6,458	United Kingdom 4,201	Canada 4,087

Total state population: 4,877,185
Total foreign-born: 59,114 (1%)

Where Do They Live?

The end of the twentieth century saw a continuing decline in the rural population of Tennessee. Today, about three-fifths of all Tennesseeans live in urban areas. The Nashville Basin, in Middle Tennessee, experienced the most rapid population growth in recent years, while West Tennessee experienced the slowest.

According to the 2000 Census, the metropolitan areas that include Nashville and Memphis each have populations of more than one million people. The population of Nashville's metropolitan area is the larger of the two.

▲ In the close-knit mountain communities of Tennessee, neighbors still pass the time making music together.

Heritage and Background, Tennessee — Year 2000

▶ Here's a look at the racial backgrounds of Tennesseeans today. Tennessee ranks twelfth among all U.S. states with regard to African Americans as a percentage of the population.

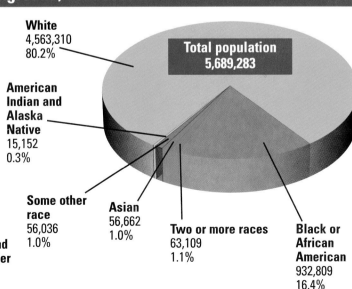

White
4,563,310
80.2%

American Indian and Alaska Native
15,152
0.3%

Some other race
56,036
1.0%

Asian
56,662
1.0%

Two or more races
63,109
1.1%

Black or African American
932,809
16.4%

Native Hawaiian and other Pacific Islander
2,205
0.04%

Total population
5,689,283

Note: 2.2% (123,838) of the population identify themselves as **Hispanic** or **Latino,** a cultural designation that crosses racial lines. Hispanics and Latinos are counted in this category as well as the racial category of their choice.

The Knoxville metropolitan area in East Tennessee has a population of more than 687,000 people, followed by the Chattanooga area and the Tri-City area of Johnson City–Kingsport–Bristol. Nearly four million people, or 70 percent of Tennessee's population, live in these five metropolitan areas.

Education

Tennessee became one of the first southern states to enact a school-attendance law, in 1913. Education continues to be a priority for Tennesseeans today, with several new programs put into place in recent years to increase the quality of education throughout the state. With 138 public school systems operating during the 2000–2001 school year, the state employed 56,588 teachers to educate 896,556 students, a student/teacher ratio of 15.8 to 1. The state spends nearly $4.5 billion per year on education. The "Better Schools" program is a respected model for the reform of public education in the nation. The program includes an increased sales tax to provide more funding to the state's schools and a system of report cards to evaluate school districts. The program also expands math and science education in the state.

Today, 67 percent of the population over the age of twenty-five have a high school diploma, while 15.7 percent have an undergraduate or more advanced college degree. There are many prestigious colleges and universities in Tennessee. The first two institutions of higher learning in the state, Blount College in Knoxville and Tusculum College in Greeneville,

▼ Nashville, the state's most populous metropolitan area and a cultural center, at night.

were both founded in 1794. Blount College later became the University of Tennessee, which now has eleven campuses in the state. Fisk University in Nashville, established in 1866, is one of the oldest African-American colleges. Other highly regarded institutions include Vanderbilt University and Tennessee State University, both in Nashville, and the University of the South, in Sewanee. The respected Jean and Alexander Heard Library and the Eskind Biomedical Library are both located at Vanderbilt University, and the Special Collection at Fisk University is a major national resource for the study of the African-American experience.

▲ Jubilee Hall at Fisk University. Fisk is home to the Carl Van Vechten Art Gallery. The university is also famous for the Jubilee Singers, a choir whose members have performed to appreciative audiences throughout the world since 1871.

Religion

The early settlers of Tennessee were mostly Protestant Christians. Today, a little more than 90 percent of Tennessee residents are Christian, and more than 43 percent are Baptist. An additional 27 percent are Southern Baptist. The state has a wide diversity of Christian denominations, including Methodist, Pentecostal, Presbyterian, Jehovah's Witness, and Seventh Day Adventist. About 4 percent of the population is Catholic. Among Tennesseeans who are not Christian are the 0.1 percent who are Muslim, 0.1 percent who are Buddhist, and 0.3 percent who are Jewish.

Tennessee is sometimes referred to as the "buckle of the Bible Belt" because of its place at the heart of Christian fundamentalism in the South.

Educational Levels of Tennessee Workers (age 25 and over)	
Less than 9th grade	500,929
9th to 12th grade, no diploma	532,985
High school graduate, including equivalency	942,865
Some college, no degree or associate degree	661,296
Bachelor's degree	330,742
Graduate or professional degree	170,249

Wild Tennessee

> Where could you find a meadow
> With grass so vividly green?
> Where could you find the mountains
> With such majestic scene?
>
> — *"Tennessee," one of Tennessee's official state songs,*
> *by Vivian Rorie*

The geography of Tennessee has influenced the diversity of the state's economy, culture, and place in history. Glaciers and other natural phenomena shaped three distinct regions — East, Middle, and West Tennessee — long before people inhabited the area. Today, each region has its own major metropolitan center and unique cultural flavor.

East Tennessee, bordered by the Appalachian Mountains to the east, is home to the Great Smoky Mountains and Clingmans Dome, the highest point in the state. It is an area of rugged terrain and forests. Until the twentieth century, East Tennessee was somewhat isolated from the rest of Tennessee. To the west, the land slopes gradually downward, with rich farmland located in valleys that stretch between the Appalachians and an area called the Cumberland Plateau. The Tennessee River flows through these valleys, and Knoxville, the state's third-largest city, is located there. The Cumberland Plateau is an area of valleys between flat-topped mountains.

Highest Point
Clingmans Dome
6,643 feet (2,025 meters)
above sea level

▼ *From left to right:* the Doe River covered bridge; Pigeon Forge Mill in East Tennessee; a black bear; wild rhododendron; Center Hill Lake; the Great Smoky Mountains.

Nashville, the state capital, is located in Middle Tennessee. It sits on the Cumberland River, which cuts a wide *U* through the northern part of this section of the state. Nashville is in a region called the Central, or Nashville, Basin, a low-lying area surrounded by higher land called the Highland Rim. The Central Basin is home to rich farmland, while the high plains that form the Highland Rim are dotted with many of the three thousand caves found in Tennessee. The Tennessee River, which flows from East Tennessee into Alabama and then loops back into West Tennessee, forms a western border for this section of the state. The rolling landscape and many rivers of Middle Tennessee allowed for the development of numerous transportation routes and a varied economy.

To the west of the Tennessee River lies West Tennessee, a region that is part of the Gulf Coastal Plain. The land there is flat and low, especially along the Mississippi River, which forms the western border of the state. Memphis, the largest city in the state, is located there. Farms, especially those raising cotton and soybeans, prosper in West Tennessee because of the area's rich soil. The economy and culture of this region have strong ties to southern states such as Mississippi and Arkansas.

The Climate

The climate is mild in Tennessee, with cool winters and warm summers. The mountains of East Tennessee experience the coldest temperatures. Rainfall is ample, and it falls fairly evenly across all regions and throughout the year.

Rivers and Lakes

The Tennessee River Basin, a *U*-shaped area running from East Tennessee to the center of the western part of the state, is made up of more than 8,300 miles (13,355 km)

Average January temperature
Memphis: 40°F (4.4°C)
Knoxville: 36°F (2.2°C)

Average July temperature
Memphis: 83°F (28.3°C)
Knoxville: 77°F (25°C)

Average yearly rainfall
Memphis: 40 inches (101.6 cm)
Knoxville: 36 inches (91.4 cm)

Average yearly snowfall
Memphis: 5.3 inches (13.5 cm)
Knoxville: 11.4 inches (28.9 cm)

Largest Lakes

Kentucky Lake
160,300 acres (64,873 ha)

Lake Barkley
57,920 acres (23,440 ha)

Watts Bar Lake
38,600 (15,621 ha)

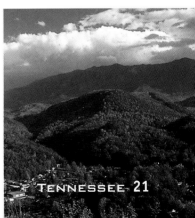

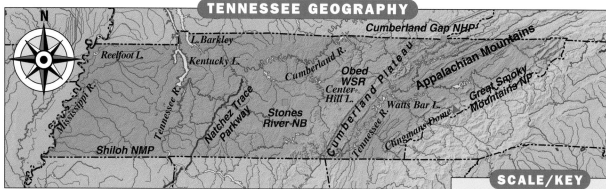

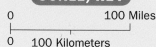

of rivers and streams. The three major rivers that travel through Tennessee are both important natural resources and vital highways for commerce. The Mississippi River forms Tennessee's westernmost border. It was a major commercial route during the nineteenth century, and it continues to play an important role in the economy of West Tennessee today. The portion of the Tennessee River that lies in the eastern part of the state exits the state to the south and then curves back up into western Tennessee, flowing north as it heads into Kentucky. The Cumberland River, which flows east to west, loops across the top of the state between the two sections of the Tennessee River. The damming of the Tennessee and Cumberland Rivers by the Tennessee Valley Authority created a series of lakes, sometimes referred to as the Great Lakes of the South, the largest of which is Kentucky Lake. Reelfoot Lake, formed by the New Madrid earthquakes in 1811–1812, is the state's largest natural lake; it is located in West Tennessee.

In the 1970s, the construction of the Tellico Dam in Lenoir City became a national issue. The dam threatened to destroy the only known habitat of the snail darter, an endangered species of small fish. In 1978, the U.S. Supreme Court decided that under the Endangered Species Act (ESA), construction on the dam could not be finished. The next year, however, U.S. senator Howard Baker and U.S. representative John Duncan, Sr., both from Tennessee, had legislation passed by the U.S. Congress that exempted the dam from the ESA. The dam was completed, and the snail darter population vanished. Several years later, small populations of the fish were discovered in other parts of the state.

DID YOU KNOW?

The New Madrid earthquakes in 1811–1812 are considered to be among the worst in U.S. history. The quakes caused a tidal wave on the Mississippi River that created Reelfoot Lake in northwestern Tennessee.

Plants

About half of the state is covered by forests, in which a variety of trees — more than two hundred species — can be found, including beech, elm, hickory, locust, maple, oak, pine, poplar, red cedar, spruce, sycamore, tulip, and walnut. Tennessee is one of the leading producers of hardwood lumber in the country. Common shrubs include azaleas, rhododendron, and mountain laurel. Flowering trees such as dogwood and magnolias are found throughout the state.

Among the wildflowers that are found in Tennessee fields are the Flanders poppy, Shasta daisy, dame's rocket, blanketflower, and clasping coneflower. Since 1993, the Department of Transportation has planted about 700 acres (283 ha) of wildflowers along the state's roadsides as part of a beautification project.

Major Rivers
Mississippi River
2,340 miles (3,765 km)

Cumberland River
720 miles (1,158 km)

Tennessee River
652 miles (1,049 km)

▼ A tree-lined road in Cades Cove, part of the Great Smoky Mountains National Park.

Animals

The varied landscapes of Tennessee have created favorable habitats for a wide variety of animals, including black bears, in the mountainous areas. Among the state's wild residents are hogs, brought to the area from Eastern Europe around 1912. The hogs, which have coarse gray hair and small sharp tusks, have become something of a menace in the region. In the Great Smoky Mountains National Park, hogs dig up plants and cause erosion by creating holes in which to wallow. They also "hog" wild foods upon which other animal populations depend. Smaller wild animals — raccoons, rabbits, skunks, foxes, and beavers — live in the forests of the region, which they share with birds such as wild ducks, geese, pheasant, and quail. Tennessee songbirds include the mockingbird (the official state bird) as well as cardinals and robins. The region around Reelfoot Lake has the largest population of bald eagles in the country. Along with other bodies of water throughout the state, the lake is home to an abundance of fish, including largemouth bass, trout, and catfish.

Riches from the Soil

> The fertile soil of Tennessee grew more than corn, tobacco and cotton. It grew a crop of people who are Trailblazers.
>
> — *Margaret Britton Vaughn, Tennessee Poet Laureate,*
> *"Who We Are," 1997*

The abundant natural resources of Tennessee, including the fertile valleys, the wildlife, and especially the rivers that flow throughout the state, all played a major role in the early economic development of the region and continue to play a role today. Long before the cities of Knoxville, Chattanooga, Nashville, and Memphis were established on the banks of the Tennessee, Cumberland, and Mississippi Rivers, the Native peoples of the area had settled along those same shores. The wealth of fish and wildlife, and the profits to be made from trading furs, were what lured these Native Americans to Tennessee, as well as the European settlers who followed them.

Today, Tennessee's economic success springs as much from technology and innovation as from river access and resources. Federal Express, one of the most successful business enterprises of modern times, got its start in 1973 in Memphis, which is still the site of this company's global headquarters. Chemical and manufacturing companies such as DuPont, Eastman-Kodak, and Aluminum Company of America (ALCOA) have also played a role in the state's economy by establishing factories in Tennessee.

Natural Riches

Coal mining has been a staple industry in Tennessee since the end of the nineteenth century. While coal mining today only accounts for 13 percent of Tennessee's mineral production, the coal that is produced in the state is of particularly fine quality. New coal reserves in the western part of the state, a source of prospective future revenues, remain untapped.

Top Employers (of workers age sixteen and over)	
Services	29.4%
Manufacturing	23.3%
Wholesale and retail trade	21.3%
Transportation, communications, and other public utilities	7.6%
Construction	6.3%
Finance, insurance, and real estate	5.3%
Public Administration	4.2%
Agriculture, forestry, and fisheries	2.3%
Mining	0.3%

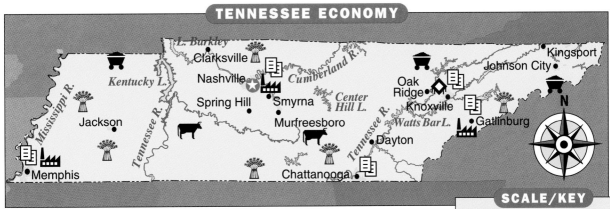

Nearly half of Tennessee's land area is farmland — 11.9 million acres of it. While farming plays a smaller role in the state's economy than it once did, such advances as precision farming, in which satellite technology increases crop yields, have made Tennessee's farming much more efficient. In the 1960s, each Tennessee farmer supplied the annual nutritional needs of 25.8 persons in the United States and abroad. Today, one farmer supplies food for 129 people.

Beef cattle are the major source of farm income in Tennessee today, with tobacco as the chief money crop, followed by hay, cotton, and corn, respectively. Tennessee is also one of the nation's top providers of hardwood. Horses are another major asset for the state — in fact, only Texas and California have more horses on their farms. Tennessee has a long tradition in this area, and has even lent its name to the Tennessee Walking Horse, the only breed of horse named for a state.

SCALE/KEY

| 0 | 100 Miles |
| 0 | 100 Kilometers |

🐂 Cattle
🌾 Farming
🏭 Manufacturing
🛒 Mining
📑 Services
◈ Technology
　 Urban Areas

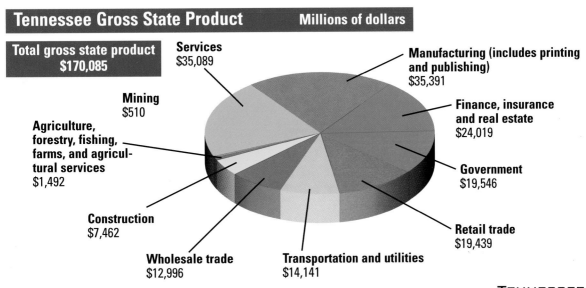

Tennessee Gross State Product — Millions of dollars

Total gross state product $170,085

- Services $35,089
- Manufacturing (includes printing and publishing) $35,391
- Mining $510
- Finance, insurance and real estate $24,019
- Agriculture, forestry, fishing, farms, and agricultural services $1,492
- Government $19,546
- Construction $7,462
- Retail trade $19,439
- Wholesale trade $12,996
- Transportation and utilities $14,141

River Power

The same rivers and streams that attracted Native Americans and early European settlers to the region eventually became the dynamo that still drives Tennessee's manufacturing power.

The Tennessee Valley Authority (TVA), established in 1933, jump-started Tennessee's economy during the Great Depression and put people back to work. The TVA was created to develop the Tennessee River Valley by building hydroelectric dams and other power plants to turn the power of the river into a commodity for the state. By 1945, the TVA was the largest producer of electricity in the United States and a powerful magnet for technology and manufacturing companies in search of cheap power. It continues to attract business today.

Modern Times

During World War II, Tennessee had a role in the creation of the first atomic bomb at a laboratory in Oak Ridge near the Tennessee River. Later, the U.S. government would choose Tennessee as the site for the Atomic Energy Commission, which was created in 1947 and lasted until 1975. This commission, which was the predecessor of the U.S. Department of Energy, was the first government agency to perform both research and promotion for a technology. This legacy of involvement in nuclear science has given technology an important place in Tennessee's economic profile. East Tennessee's Knoxville/Oak Ridge Technology Corridor, which includes the University of

Made in Tennessee

Leading farm products and crops

Cattle and calves
Tobacco
Hay
Cotton
Corn
Horses
Dairy products
Poultry
Fruits and vegetables
Hogs
Soybeans

Other products

Hardwood lumber
Chemicals
Fabricated metals
Industrial and
    commercial machinery
Electronics
Rubber and plastics
Furniture
Transportation equipment

Major Airports

Airport	Location	Passengers per year (2000)
Memphis International	Memphis	11,760,213
Nashville International	Nashville	9,044,065

Tennessee and the Oak Ridge National Laboratory, is an internationally renowned center for the research and development of new technologies. The area contains over five hundred high-tech companies.

Since 1960, more people have lived in Tennessee's cities than rural areas. The electrical power generated by the TVA, which is still in force, has attracted industries as diverse as chemical and apparel manufacturing. In 1980, with the selection of Smyrna as the site of a new Nissan truck assembly plant, the state experienced an influx of automobile manufacturing companies, including a General Motors Saturn plant in Spring Hill that opened in 1990.

The rich cultural history of Tennessee has helped to create an $8.5 billion tourist industry to complement the manufacturing industry. Music is also one of Tennessee's economic powerhouses, with the country music mecca of Nashville and its Country Music Hall of Fame and Museum feeding the state's multi-billion-dollar industry.

DID YOU KNOW?

The Oak Ridge National Laboratory, established in 1943 to develop an atomic bomb, was the site of the first continuously operating nuclear reactor in the world.

▼ The coal industry has long been important to Tennessee's economy. At this plant in Kingsport, coal is processed into gas for a variety of uses.

The Sixteenth State

> I will neither keep house, nor make butter...I always take a deep interrest [*sic*] in State and national affairs.
>
> — *Sarah Childress Polk, wife of President James K. Polk*

T he first Tennessee state constitution was written in Knoxville and adopted in 1796. It was approved by the U.S. Congress but not by the voters of the region, and, as a result, a second constitutional convention was called in Nashville in 1834. A new constitution was written and ratified (approved) by the people of Tennessee in 1835. The constitution was again rewritten and ratified in 1870. This document is still in effect today, along with amendments passed in 1953, 1960, 1966, 1972, 1978, and 1998.

Tennessee's constitution divides the state government into executive, legislative, and judicial branches. Amendments to the constitution may be proposed in the state senate or house of representatives and must be agreed to by a majority of all members of both houses. The amendment must then be published for six months. Next, it must be passed by a two-thirds vote of all members of both houses at the next General Assembly meeting. If the amendment passes in the General Assembly, it must be proposed to the people of Tennessee at the next general election. The amendment becomes law only if it is approved by a majority of people who also cast a vote for the governor in that election.

The legislature may also call for a constitutional convention at any general election, and this proposal must be passed by a majority of qualified voters.

Executive Branch

The governor of Tennessee, the chief executive officer of the state, is elected for a four-year term and must be at least thirty years old. The governor, who may serve a maximum of two consecutive terms, oversees an administrative branch of twenty-two departments headed by commissioners appointed by the governor. The governor's

---

State Constitution

That all power is inherent in the people, and all free governments are founded on their authority, and instituted for their peace, safety, and happiness; for the advancement of those ends they have at all times, an inalienable and indefeasible right to alter, reform, and abolish the government in such manner as they may think proper.

— *from the Tennessee Constitution of 1870*

cabinet is made up of commissioners of the largest of these departments, as well as senior staff assistants.

Every bill that passes both houses of the General Assembly must be given to the governor for his or her signature. The General Assembly, however, has the right to override the governor's veto by a majority vote of both houses.

Legislative Branch

The General Assembly of the state of Tennessee consists of a senate and a house of representatives, members of which are elected by the people of the state. There are thirty-three senators, who serve four-year terms, and ninety-nine representatives, who serve two-year terms. The General Assembly convenes on the second Tuesday of January in each odd-numbered year. The governor may call a special session of the General Assembly, as can members of the legislature. The General Assembly enacts, amends, and repeals laws. It can also impose taxes and authorize expenditures of funds from the state treasury. The lieutenant governor is elected by the state senate, while the secretary of state and the treasurer are elected by a joint vote of the General Assembly.

Founding Father

Born in Overton, Cordell Hull (1871–1955) served in the U.S. House and Senate before President Franklin Roosevelt appointed him secretary of state in 1933. Hull served in this post until 1944 — longer than any secretary of state before or since. Hull strongly supported the creation of an organization to settle international disputes peacefully — an effort that won him the nickname "The Father of the United Nations." He was awarded the Nobel Peace Prize in 1945.

▼ The Tennessee state capitol building, on the right, was built in 1859. It stands on the Legislative Plaza with other government buildings.

Elected Post in the Executive Branch		
Office	Length of Term	Term Limits
Governor	4 years	2 consecutive terms

Judicial Branch

Tennessee's highest court is the supreme court. It reviews civil and criminal cases that are appealed from lower courts and decides matters having to do with state taxes, constitutional issues, and the right to hold office. The court also names the state attorney general (called, in Tennessee, the attorney general and reporter), who serves an eight-year term. The Tennessee Supreme Court consists of five justices, who are elected to eight-year terms. The justices designate one of their members as chief justice. No more than two of the five justices can reside in each of the state's three "grand divisions" (East, Middle, and West Tennessee). The court meets on a rotating basis in Knoxville, Nashville, and Jackson.

There are twelve judges on the state court of appeals, which hears appeals of civil (noncriminal) cases from lower state courts. Cases are heard by panels of three judges. The court of criminal appeals hears appeals of verdicts in criminal trials. This court also consists of twelve judges who work in panels of three.

Tennessee has thirty-one judicial districts, each with a circuit court and a chancery court. Judges for these courts are popularly elected and serve eight-year terms. Most circuit courts try both civil and criminal cases, but there are some judicial districts with separate criminal courts. Circuit courts may also hear appeals from local courts. The chancery courts hear cases in which unusual types of relief are sought, such as a particular exception to the way a law is applied.

Politics

The political leanings of the state of Tennessee have changed over time. Solidly Democratic for the years following the Civil War (with the exception of East Tennessee, which was more allied with the Republican party), Tennessee now supports candidates of both parties in both local and national elections.

General Assembly			
House	Number of Members	Length of Term	Term Limits
Senate	33 senators	4 years	None
House of Representatives	99 representatives	2 years	None

ANDREW JACKSON (1829–1837)

A member of the early Democratic party, Andrew Jackson was born in South Carolina in 1767. He moved to Tennessee at age twenty-one to practice law. He was a hero of the War of 1812 and earned the nickname "Old Hickory" for his toughness during battle. Jackson helped write Tennessee's first constitution and served Tennessee in both the U.S. House of Representatives and the Senate. He was elected as the seventh president of the United States in 1828 and served two terms.

Jackson was called "the People's President," because of his humble background and concern for common citizens. Major issues during his two terms were the rights of individual states versus those of the central government, and the legality of a national bank.

His election saw a shift of power away from the original thirteen states and toward the new western states, including Tennessee. Jackson's concern for the people of the land did not extend to the Native Americans, however. As president, he strictly enforced the measures that led to the forced migration of the Cherokee and other Native peoples from their homelands.

JAMES K. POLK (1845–1849)

A Democrat, James Knox Polk was born in North Carolina but moved to Tennessee at age eleven and grew up in the Duck River Valley. He served in the state legislature and U.S. House of Representatives

before becoming governor of Tennessee in 1839 and U.S. president in 1845. At the beginning of his term, Polk announced that he would not be running for reelection, but that he would do four major things while in office. He promised to lower the tariff, settle a border dispute with Great Britain over Oregon, acquire California, and establish an independent treasury office. He accomplished each of these things.

In 1845, when the United States annexed Texas, Mexico declared war. In the treaty that ended the Mexican War, the United States won not only California, but all of the Southwest. Polk is remembered as one of the hardest-working men ever to have been president. He died a few months after he left office.

ANDREW JOHNSON (1865–1869)

Born in North Carolina, Andrew Johnson moved to Tennessee when he was seventeen. Beginning his political career in 1830, Johnson was an alderman, mayor, state representative, governor, congressman, and senator. In 1865, he became Abraham Lincoln's vice president. That year, Lincoln was assassinated and Johnson became president. Johnson faced the difficult problem of how to rebuild the nation after the Civil War. Many politicians were dissatisfied with his plans, and, in 1868, he was impeached, although he was found not guilty and was allowed to serve out his term. In 1874, Johnson won election as a U.S. senator for Tennessee. He died several months after taking office.

Grand Ole Times

> Let's give old Tennessee credit for music
> As they play it up in Nashville everyday
> Let's give old Tennessee credit for music
> As they play it in that old hillbilly way
>
> — *Carl Perkins, from "Tennessee," 1956*

While country music and Tennessee are often thought of as synonymous, the state boasts an impressive cultural variety, including art, literature, classical music, sports, and a rich folk tradition. Tennesseeans enjoy wonderful museums, symphony orchestras, and numerous professional and amateur sporting events, as well as a variety of festivals that celebrate the region's unique history and culture. America has been enriched by the literary contributions of Tennesseeans, including several Pulitzer Prize-winning authors. This prestigious prize for literature was awarded to Alex Haley, author of *Roots*, as well as James Agee, author of *A Death in the Family*, Robert Penn Warren, author of *All the King's Men*, and Peter Taylor, author of *A Summons to Memphis*.

Craftspeople and artists in Tennessee have created a wealth of decorative art, including quilts, baskets, furniture, and folk art. The pride taken in the colorful speech and wonderful stories that have been passed down from generation to generation is celebrated in the National Storytelling Festival, held in Jonesborough each fall. The contributions of Tennessee musicians, including musical talents such as Chet Atkins, Loretta Lynn, Elvis Presley, W. C. Handy, and B. B. King, to name just a few, have left their mark on both American culture and the rest of the world.

◀ Elvis Presley, known as "the King of Rock and Roll," helped put Memphis on the musical map.

House of the Rising Sun

In 1949, Memphis disc jockey Sam Phillips opened his own recording studio. He called it Sun Studios and advertised that "we record anything — anywhere — anytime." One afternoon in 1954, a young Elvis Presley took the afternoon off from his job in a machine shop and paid Phillips $3.98 to record a song for his mother. Phillips asked Presley to record with some musicians he knew. The song they recorded, "That's All Right (Mama)," became a huge hit. Other stars who made Sun a famous studio include Carl Perkins, Johnny Cash, and Jerry Lee Lewis.

Country, Blues, and Rock and Roll

From the bluegrass of the East Tennessee mountains to the country music of Nashville in Middle Tennessee to the blues and rock of Memphis on the Mississippi River, music is certainly Tennessee's greatest contribution to American culture.

The mountain music of East Tennessee was based on traditional folk songs, brought to the area by settlers originally from England and Scotland. It was transformed over time into country music. When the Nashville radio station WSM began broadcasting a new program, eventually named the *Grand Ole Opry*, in 1925, the station featured bands with names like the Possum Hunters and the Fruit Jar Drinkers.

Far from the traditions of country music in the east, slaves in West Tennessee were singing soulful spirituals and mournful blues to help them through the tedious, hard work of their days. In the 1900s, jazz emerged from the blending of African-American folk music and European music. W. C. Handy, the composer of such songs as "Beale Street Blues" and "Memphis Blues," brought together blues and jazz to create his own unique rhythm-and-blues style. Just as Nashville became the home of country music, Memphis established itself as a center of jazz and blues, and the music industry began to flourish in both cities.

▼ Onstage at the Grand Ole Opry House in Nashville, where many famous names in country music had their first big break.

The popularity of the country music coming out of Tennessee increased after World War II, and the *Grand Ole Opry* was broadcast throughout the United States. Rock and roll was born in the 1950s, when Elvis Presley combined the sounds of country and western music with that of rhythm and blues.

Music fans came to Tennessee in increasing numbers, and a variety of museums and tourist destinations were created to satisfy their wish to learn more about the music industry. The Country Music Hall of Fame and Museum in Nashville opened in 1967 and moved to a new and grander facility in 2001. A tour through the museum gives the history of country music, and features exhibits of memorabilia from Jimmy Rodgers, Minnie Pearl, and scores of other country stars. In 1974, "Opryland" opened. Based on the popularity of the *Grand Ole Opry* radio program, it is a music theme park and venue for the performance of live music in Nashville. Graceland, Elvis's home in Memphis, was opened to the public in 1982 and is the biggest tourist attraction in the city. Fans from all over the world come to Graceland, especially during the weeks that mark the anniversary of Elvis's birth and death.

▲ The Country Music Hall of Fame and Museum has a fascinating collection of musical instruments, costumes, and memorabilia from the careers of country music's biggest stars.

Great Smoky Outdoors

Tennessee is famous for its beautiful mountain scenery. There are more than fifty state parks and nine national parks, historic sites, and recreation areas. The most famous of these is the Great Smoky Mountains National Park, which covers more than 521,000 acres (210,849 ha) in North Carolina and Tennessee. The park is forested over 95 percent of its area. Within the park, Cades Cove, a 6,800-acre (2,752-ha) area, offers visitors a collection of nineteenth-century buildings as well as natural scenery. The Mountain Farm Museum in the park is a collection of farm buildings that have been preserved to reflect mountain life in the nineteenth century. Visitors may also travel the park's trails by foot, bicycle, or horseback.

Cove Lake State Park is a 673-acre (272-ha) area in the Cumberland Mountains where visitors may hike along nature trails through forests and grasslands and beside a mountain lake. Nearby, Devil's Race Trace is a mountain peak that offers views in all directions.

The Hermitage

Near Nashville is the stately, columned house that was Andrew Jackson's home for the latter part of his life. He bought the land in 1804 and lived in a log cabin on the grounds for many years before building a brick house. The house that stands today was built in 1836, after a fire destroyed the first brick house. In addition to the house itself, visitors to the Hermitage can see the original log cabin, a slave house, and Jackson's tomb and the family cemetery.

Cumberland Mountain State Park, on 1,720 acres (696 ha), is part of the Cumberland Plateau, an area that stretches all the way from New York to Alabama. The park was opened in 1938 as part of the New Deal. Roan Mountain State Park, in the northeastern corner of the state, enjoys an abundance of wildflowers each spring, as well as cool evenings for summer campers. This area has the longest stretch of grassy balds — treeless, grass-covered, knoblike peaks — in the United States.

Museums and Historic Sites

The major cities of Tennessee all contain fine art museums with world-class collections, as well as many historical museums. In Chattanooga, the Hunter Museum of American Art houses an impressive collection of nineteenth- and twentieth-century art, including works by Ansel Adams, Alexander Calder, and Mary Cassatt. The Houston Museum of Decorative Arts, also in Chattanooga, has an astounding collection of antique glass pieces and furniture. In Nashville, the Cheekwood Botanical Garden and Museum of Art boasts an art collection and outstanding gardens, and antique portraits of Tennesseeans can be seen

Brief Utopia

In October 1880, British author Thomas Hughes, famous for his book *Tom Brown's School Days*, established a unique community in Tennessee's Cumberland Plateau. Called Rugby, this town was designed as a cooperative community of young men. The dream lasted only a few years, however, as disease, poor weather, and financial troubles all took their toll. Today, the site, which includes twenty restored buildings, is on the National Register of Historic Places and is open to visitors.

▼ A cannon sits on Lookout Mountain in the Chickamauga and Chattanooga National Military Park, on the border with Georgia.

at the Tennessee State Museum. Fisk University, also in Nashville, is home to the Carl Van Vechten Art Gallery, which features works by Alfred Stieglitz, Paul Cezanne, Pablo Picasso, and Auguste Renoir.

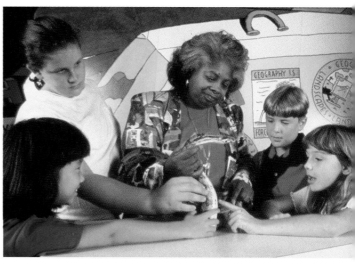

Sites celebrating the history and cultural traditions of Tennessee abound. Shiloh National Military Park and Stones River National Battlefield are both Civil War battlefields. The National Civil Rights Museum is located in Memphis's Lorraine Motel, where Martin Luther King, Jr., was assassinated. The museum tells the story of the Civil Rights Movement. Also in Memphis is the Center for Southern Folklore, dedicated to southern music, literature, and art. It features a folk art gallery and live music performances that highlight the traditions of the state.

Several artists from Tennessee have gained national attention. James Cameron, who worked in the mid-1800s, is known for his landscapes. Later in the same century, George deForest Brush, whose work appears in the collection of the Metropolitan Museum of Art in New York City, became a respected painter of Native Americans, and Frank Wilbert Stokes painted "Return of Commander Byrd and Floyd Bennet from the North Pole."

Literature and Publishing

Tennessee has a tradition of storytelling, with folk tales and country "yarns" in abundance. This storytelling tradition extends to the written word as well. The state has produced a wealth of serious writers, including Alex Haley, whose book *Roots* tells the multigenerational story of an African-American family and was made into a hugely popular television miniseries.

Tennessee's first library opened in Charlotte in 1811, and in 1813 the first public library in the state was established. Today, there are more than 250 public libraries in Tennessee. Published in 1791, the *Knoxville Gazette* was the first newspaper in the state. There are about thirty daily newspapers published in Tennessee today. Memphis's newspaper, the *Commercial Appeal*, has the state's highest circulation, followed by the *Nashville Tennesseean*, first published in 1812. Others include the *Knoxville News-Sentinel* and the *Chattanooga Times Free Press*.

Sports

Tennesseeans are loyal sports fans and take great pride in the accomplishments of their athletes. The University of Tennessee's Lady Vols basketball team won six national championships between 1987 and 1998, and the university's football team, the Volunteers, was undefeated in 1998 and was national champion. Although Tennessee does not have a professional baseball team, there are numerous minor-league teams in the state that enjoy the support of their fans. Other professional sports have arrived in Tennessee in recent years. The Houston Oilers, a National Football League (NFL) team, moved to Memphis in 1997 and then to Nashville in 1999, where they became the Tennessee Titans. In 2000, the Titans made it to the Super Bowl. The Nashville Predators have brought a National Hockey League (NHL) team to the state, and the National Basketball Association (NBA) Grizzlies made their debut in Memphis in 2001.

Sport	Team	Home
Basketball	Memphis Grizzlies	Pyramid Arena, Memphis
Football	Tennessee Titans	Adelphia Coliseum, Nashville
Hockey	Nashville Predators	Gaylord Entertainment Center, Nashville

▼ Fans cheer on the University of Tennessee football team, the Volunteers.

Trailblazers

*If you don't understand yourself
you don't understand anybody else.*
— *Nikki Giovanni, Tennessee poet, 1971*

Following are only a few of the thousands of people who were born, died, or spent much of their lives in Tennessee and made extraordinary contributions to the state and the nation.

JOHN SEVIER
POLITICAL LEADER

BORN: *September 23, 1745, New Market, VA*
DIED: *September 24, 1815, Fort Decatur,
   Mississippi Territory*

A frontiersman, soldier, and politician who did much to establish Tennessee as the sixteenth state in the Union, John Sevier moved with his family to eastern Tennessee in 1773. As a soldier during the Revolutionary War, Sevier made a name for himself at the Battle of Kings Mountain in South Carolina. He helped found the separate but unrecognized state of Franklin in 1784 and became the governor of this self-proclaimed state. When Tennessee was admitted to the Union in 1796, Sevier was

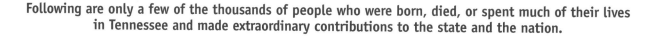

elected its first governor. He served in that post until 1801 and again from 1803 to 1809. Sevier also served as a state senator and as a member of the U.S. House of Representatives from 1811 until his death in 1815.

MINNIE PEARL
ENTERTAINER

BORN: *October 25, 1912, Centerville*
DIED: *March 4, 1996, Nashville*

Born Sarah Ophelia Colley, Minnie Pearl was one of the most beloved stars of the *Grand Ole Opry*, performing on the program for more than fifty years. The daughter of a sawmill owner in Centerville, she grew up surrounded by many small-town folks who would later influence the character she created for herself, named Minnie Pearl. Greeting audiences with her "How-dee! I'm just so proud to be here!" and a $1.98 price tag hanging from her straw hat, Pearl created a down-home image for herself and was much loved by her fans. She was elected to the Country Music Hall of Fame in 1975. She received the Courage Award from the American Cancer Society in 1987 and a National Medal of Arts in 1992.

JAMES AGEE
WRITER

BORN: *November 27, 1909, Knoxville*
DIED: *May 16, 1955, New York, NY*

James Agee grew up in rural Cumberland County and graduated from Harvard University in 1932. He became known as a writer of movie reviews and also published poetry. In 1936, *Fortune* magazine hired Agee and photographer Walker Evans to write an article about the effects of the Great Depression on the South. Agee and Evans turned their experiences of living with rural families in Alabama into a book, *Let Us Now Praise Famous Men* (1941). The book became well known as a sensitive portrayal of American poverty. Agee also wrote screenplays, including *The African Queen* and *Night of the Hunter*. His novel *A Death in the Family*, which dealt with the sudden death of his father when Agee was a child, was published after his death and won the Pulitzer Prize in 1958.

CORNELIA FORT
AVIATOR

BORN: *February 5, 1919, Nashville*
DIED: *March 21, 1943, near Merkel, Texas*

Cornelia Fort was the first woman pilot in U.S. history to die on active duty. Growing up on a Nashville farm, she was a child of social standing and privilege. A demonstration by barnstorming aviators at a country fair captured her imagination, but it wasn't until after her graduation from Sarah Lawrence College in New York and the death of her father that she took flying lessons and devoted herself to her new passion. She was in the air over Honolulu, Hawaii, when the Japanese attacked Pearl Harbor. The second woman to enlist as a pilot in World War II, Fort was a member of the Women's Auxiliary Ferrying Squadron. As part of this group, she and her fellow pilots transported training planes from factories to air bases, where male pilots were training for combat. In 1943, Fort died when her plane crashed near Merkel, Texas, during a training exercise.

ALEX HALEY
AUTHOR

BORN: *August 11, 1921, Ithaca, NY*
DIED: *February 10, 1992, Seattle, WA*

Alex Palmer Haley moved to Henning, Tennessee, with his family soon after he was born. The son of teachers, Haley grew up listening to his grandmother's and aunts' stories, and he traced the family history back to Kunta Kinte, who came to this country from Africa on a slave ship in 1767. The stories formed the basis for his best-selling novel published in 1976, titled *Roots: The Saga of an American Family*, which won the National Book Award and a Pulitzer Prize and was made into a highly successful TV miniseries in 1977. The book raised interest in tracing family histories, particularly for African Americans, and Haley helped establish the Kinte Foundation, which is dedicated to the collection and preservation of African-American genealogy records. Another work for which Haley is known is *The Autobiography of Malcolm X,* an important account of the African-American activist's life, which was published in 1965. His boyhood home, part of the Alex Haley House Museum in Henning, is open to the public.

ELVIS PRESLEY
MUSICIAN

BORN: *January 8, 1935, Tupelo, MS*
DIED: *August 16, 1977, Memphis*

Elvis Aaron Presley, "the King of Rock and Roll," grew up in poverty as an only child, his twin brother having died at birth. The Presley family moved to Memphis in 1948. Elvis was influenced by both the gospel music he heard in church and the rhythm and blues being played on historic Beale Street. In 1954, he recorded a single at Sun Studios. Sun founder Sam Phillips called him back to make another record accompanied by two other musicians, Scotty Moore and Bill Black. The resulting "That's All Right (Mama)" was on Memphis radio within days and set in motion a new era in American music and culture. Wildly popular, Elvis sold over one billion records, starred in thirty-three movies,

and performed to sold-out audiences. Some of his most famous songs include "Heartbreak Hotel" and "All Shook Up." Elvis's Memphis home, Graceland, was opened to the public in 1982, five years after his death.

WILMA RUDOLPH
ATHLETE

BORN: *June 23, 1940, St. Bethlehem*
DIED: *November 12, 1994, Nashville*

Wilma Glodean Rudolph became the first American woman runner to win three gold medals in the Olympic Games. The twentieth of twenty-two children, Rudolph became ill with polio and scarlet fever as a youngster. She was unable to use one of her legs and needed a brace to help her walk. Leg massages and determination eventually enabled her to walk unassisted. By the time she was fourteen she was running track and was undefeated in all of her high school meets. At Tennessee State University, Rudolph set the world record for the 200-meter dash, and she went on to set records in the 1960 Olympics, where she won gold medals in the 100-meter dash, the 200-meter dash, and as the anchor for the 400-meter relay. She was named the United Press Athlete of the Year in 1960, and she won the Amateur Athletic Union's Sullivan Award in 1961. She founded the Wilma Rudolph Foundation for the promotion of community track and field programs in 1962 and was inducted into the National Track and Field Hall of Fame, the International Women's Sports Hall of Fame, and the U.S. Olympic Hall of Fame.

Nikki Giovanni
POET

BORN: *June 7, 1943, Knoxville*

Born in Knoxville, Nikki Giovanni was mostly raised in Cincinnati, Ohio. She later attended Fisk University, a predominately African-American college, where she became involved in both writing and campus protest, joining both the Writer's Workshop and the Student Non-Violent Coordinating Committee. Giovanni's poetry reflected her experiences as a black woman in a white-dominated society. In 1967 she joined other radical African-American poets as part of the Black Arts movement, as politics and then single motherhood began to have a deeper influence on her poetry. Among her major works are *Black Feeling, Black Talk* (1968) and *Sacred Cows...and Other Edibles* (1988). Currently, Nikki Giovanni is a professor at Virginia Tech, where she teaches English.

Dolly Parton
SINGER/SONGWRITER

BORN: *January 19, 1946, Locust Ridge*

Dolly Rebecca Parton grew up on a farm in rural East Tennessee and began singing on the radio when she was still a child. In 1966, she joined the cast of Porter Wagoner's TV show. Among the first of her many big hits was "Coat of Many Colors," which recalled the poor but happy days of her childhood. She has also performed in several movies. In 1987, Parton made "Trio," a recording with Emmylou Harris and Linda Rondstadt that won a Grammy Award. She has won four other Grammy Awards and seven Country Music Association awards. Parton was inducted into the Country Music Hall of Fame in 1999.

Albert Gore, Jr.
POLITICIAN

BORN: *March 31, 1948, Washington, DC*

Albert Arnold Gore, Jr., is considered a Tennesseean even though he spent much of his childhood in Washington, D.C. After graduating from Harvard, Gore served in the Vietnam War. In 1971, he returned home to Tennessee to work for a Nashville newspaper. He was elected to the U.S. House of Representatives in 1976 and won a seat in the Senate in 1984. Bill Clinton chose Gore as his running mate in 1992, and Gore became vice president in 1993. He served with Clinton for a second term and was the Democratic presidential nominee in the 2000 election against George W. Bush. One of the most controversial elections in history followed, with Gore winning the popular vote but apparently losing the Electoral College by a slim margin. Ultimately, after a period of five weeks, during which the nation waited for a resolution to the controversy, the U.S. Supreme Court voted to avoid a recount of disputed voter ballots, and Bush won the election. Known as a moderate Democrat, Gore is a champion of the environment and technology and a supporter of gun control and women's rights.

Tennessee

History At-A-Glance

1540
Hernando de Soto of Spain is the first European to explore the Tennessee region.

1673
British explorers Gabriel Arthur and James Needham come to the Tennessee River Valley.

1682
René-Robert Cavelier, Sieur de La Salle, claims the Mississippi River Valley, including Tennessee, for France.

1714
French Lick, a French trading post, is established near present-day Nashville.

1750
Thomas Walker discovers the Cumberland Gap, through which the Wilderness Trail will be carved to allow settlers into the region.

1772
The Wautauga Association, an early example of colonial self-government, is formed.

1775
Transylvania Purchase is signed, allowing for the transfer of millions of acres of land from the Cherokee to the settlers.

1780
Fort Nashborough, later Nashville, is established.

1796
Tennessee becomes the sixteenth state. John Sevier becomes the first governor.

1818
A treaty with the Chickasaw gives more land to settlers.

1828
Andrew Jackson is elected the seventh president of the United States.

1835
The forced removal of the Cherokee from Tennessee, known as the "Trail of Tears," begins.

1600　　　　**1700**　　　　**1800**

1492
Christopher Columbus comes to New World.

1607
Capt. John Smith and three ships land on Virginia coast and start first English settlement in New World — Jamestown.

1754–63
French and Indian War.

1773
Boston Tea Party.

1776
Declaration of Independence adopted July 4.

1777
Articles of Confederation adopted by Continental Congress.

1787
U.S. Constitution written.

1812–14
War of 1812.

United States

History At-A-Glance

1844
Tennesseean James K. Polk is elected the eleventh president.

1861
Tennessee votes to secede from the Union.

1865
Andrew Johnson becomes the seventeenth president.

1920
The 19th Amendment to the U.S. Constitution, giving women the right to vote, becomes law when it is ratified by the Tennessee legislature.

1925
The *Grand Ole Opry* is first broadcast from Nashville. The Scopes trial takes place in Dayton.

1933
The Tennessee Valley Authority (TVA) is formed by President Franklin Roosevelt.

1934
The Great Smoky Mountains National Park is established.

1943
Construction begins on laboratories in Oak Ridge as part of the Manhattan Project, the U.S. effort to create an atomic bomb.

1964
A. W. Willis, Jr., is the first African American elected to the state legislature.

1968
Martin Luther King, Jr., is assassinated in Memphis.

1982
Automobile manufacturing becomes a major industry in Tennessee with the establishment of a Nissan plant in Smyrna.

Knoxville is home to a World's Fair.

1800   **1900**   **2000**

1848
Gold discovered in California draws eighty thousand prospectors in the 1849 Gold Rush.

1861–65
Civil War.

1869
Transcontinental railroad completed.

1917–18
U.S. involvement in World War I.

1929
Stock market crash ushers in Great Depression.

1941–45
U.S. involvement in World War II.

1950–53
U.S. fights in the Korean War.

1964–73
U.S. involvement in Vietnam War.

2000
George W. Bush wins the closest presidential election in history.

2001
A terrorist attack in which four hijacked airliners crash into New York City's World Trade Center, the Pentagon, and farmland in western Pennsylvania leaves thousands dead or injured.

▼ **Construction of a bridge over the Tennessee River at Chattanooga in 1917.**

Festivals and Fun for All

Check web site for exact date and directions.

Anniversary of the Battle of Shiloh, Shiloh National Military Park, Shiloh

This event commemorates the anniversary of the Battle of Shiloh, which took place on April 6–7, 1862. There are three days of battle reenactments, with authentic Civil War-era costumes. The Battle of Shiloh was an important victory for the Union.
www.shiloh140th.com

Cherokee Days of Recognition, Cleveland

This event is held in August near the place where Cherokee councils were held in the 1830s. It includes Native American dances, games, authentic Cherokee crafts and foods, and a blowgun tournament.
www.state.tn.us/environment/parks/redclay/events.htm

Cosby Ramp Festival, Cosby

A ramp is a strong, onion-flavored plant that grows wild in the eastern United States. Locals and visitors alike mark the arrival of ramp season with bluegrass and gospel music that accompanies true country cooking in the best mountain style.
www.cockecounty.com

A Day of Remembrance, Memphis

Held each April at the National Civil Rights Museum, this event marks the anniversary of the assassination of Dr. Martin Luther King, Jr., on April 4, 1968.
www.civilrightsmuseum.org

Dogwood Arts Festival, Knoxville

Knoxville's dogwood trees are in full bloom in April. To celebrate, there is a month-long festival, which includes the Foothills Craft Guild Show; art, photography, and quilt shows; the Dogwood Arts Festival Parade; a three-night concert series; a folk art festival; a tennis tournament; the Dogwood Grand Prix; the Fountain City festival; ballet performers; and more.
www.dogwoodarts.com

Elvis Week, Memphis

Elvis Presley fans from all over the world gather in August, on the anniversary of his death, to celebrate the musical legacy of "the King." The week's many events take place all over the city. They include many musical performances, of course, as well as dance parties, sporting events, and charitable fundraisers.
www.elvis.com

Fan Fair, Nashville

Held in June at the Adelphia Coliseum, Riverfront Park, and the Nashville Convention Center, Fan Fair is a weekend of musical celebration for fans of country music. There are stage shows and other musical events, as well as picture and autograph sessions at which fans get to meet their favorite country music stars.
www.fanfair.com

▼ National Storytelling Festival.

July 4th Celebration and Anvil Shoot, Norris

Held at the Museum of Appalachia, this event celebrates the 4th of July with activities and fireworks, highlighted by the launching of a 150-pound (68-kg) anvil into the air.
www.museumofappalachia.com

Memphis in May International Festival, Memphis

This month-long celebration highlights the musical and culinary heritage of Memphis, with concerts and a barbecue-cooking contest. One week of the celebration is devoted to the culture of another country, with food, crafts, and entertainment.
www.memphisinmay.org

Mule Day, Columbia

Mule Day is actually a week of festivities in honor of this hard-working animal. The celebration has its origins in the mid-nineteenth-century mule market held each year in Columbia. The modern event features food, a flea market, live entertainment, and, of course, mule shows.
www.muleday.com

National Cornbread Festival, South Pittsburg

Visitors to Tennessee in late April can enjoy this festival celebrating cornbread and small-town Southern hospitality.
www.nationalcornbread.com

National Storytelling Festival, Jonesborough

Held the first weekend in October, this festival is famed around the world as the premier storytelling event in America.
www.storytellingcenter.net

Scopes Trial Play & Festival, Dayton

Held in July at the Rhea County Courthouse, this event is a reenactment of the 1925 Scopes "Monkey Trial," held in the original courthouse.
www.rheacounty.com

Smithville Fiddlers' Jamboree and Crafts Festival, Smithville

Fiddlers from around the nation gather in Smithville in early July to compete for the grand prize awarded at the end of the jamboree. Audiences of up to one hundred thousand are treated not only to two days of lively music, but also to a crafts show that honors Appalachian culture.
www.smithvilletn.com

Tennessee Walking Horse National Celebration, Shelbyville

In late August, this famous horse breed — native to Tennessee — is celebrated through exhibitions and the selection of the Grand Champion Tennessee Walking Horse of the Year.
www.twhnc.com

West Tennessee Strawberry Festival, Humboldt

West Tennessee strawberries are at their peak in early May, just in time for the festival. Some of the many events that take place during the week-long celebration are a recipe contest, a pet parade, a carnival, and an art show.
www.humboldtchamber. tn.org /strawberry.htm

Books

Biracree, Tom. *Wilma Rudolph (American Women of Achievement)*. Minneapolis, MN: Econo-Clad, 1999. A look at the life of Olympic track star Wilma Rudolph, who overcame polio to win three Olympic gold medals.

Harmon, Daniel E. *Davy Crockett*. New York: Chelsea House, 2001. A biography of the famous frontiersman and politician.

Kent, Deborah. *Tennessee*. New York: Children's Press, 2001. Facts and figures about the state of Tennessee.

Oppenheim, Joanne. *Sequoyah: Cherokee Hero*. Minneapolis, MN: Econo-Clad Books, 1999. This biography tells about the life and achievements of a famous Native American.

Stewart, Gail B. *The Tennessee Walking Horse*. Mankato, MN: Capstone Press, 1996. This book discusses the history and special features of one of the most famous breeds of horses in the world.

Watkins, Sam R. *Company Aytch*. New York: Dutton Plume, 1999. The Civil War memories of a Tennessee college student who fought for the Confederacy and wrote about his experiences.

Web Sites

▶ Official state web site
www.state.tn.us

▶ Official web site of the state capital
www.nashville.gov

▶ Web site of the Tennessee Historical Commission
www.state.tn.us/environment/hist

Note: Page numbers in *italics* refer to illustrations, maps, or photographs.

A

African Americans, 13–15, 19, 36, 39–40
age distribution, 16
Agee, James, 4, 8, 32, 39
agriculture, 4, 11–12, 20, 21, 25, 26
airports, 27
animals of Tennessee, 4, 6, 7, *20*, 23
Anniversary of the Battle of Shiloh, 44
Appalachian Mountains, 9, 20
architecture, 7, *29*, 37
area of state, 6
Arthur, Gabriel, 8
Atkins, Chet, 32
Atomic Energy Commission, 26–27
Attakullakulla (Cherokee leader), 9
attractions, 7, 32, 44–45
auto industry, 27

B

Baker, Howard, 22
basketball, 37
Battle of Kings Mountain, 10
Battle of Murfreesboro, 12
Battle of New Orleans, *10*
Battle of Shiloh, 12, *13*, 44
Bean, William, 9
birds, 6, 23
Blount, William, 8, 10
Blount College, 18
bluegrass music, 33
blues music, 33
Boone, Daniel, 9
bridges, *20*
Bristol, Tennessee, 18
Brush, George deForest, 36
Bryan, William Jennings, 14

C

Cades Cove, 23, 34
Cameron, James, 36
candies, 7
capitals, 6, 11, 21
capitol building, *29*
Carl Van Vechten Art Gallery, 35
cattle, 25
Cavelier, René-Robert (de La Salle), 8
Center for Southern Folklore, 36
Center Hill Lake, *21*
Central Basin, 21
Charleville, Charles, 8

Chattanooga, Tennessee, 6, 12, 18, 24, 35, *42–43*
Chattanooga National Military Park, 35
chemical industry, 24
Cherokee Days of Recognition, 44
Cherokee Indians, 8–11, 31
Cherokee Phoenix, 11
Chickamauga and Chattanooga National Military Park, 35
Chickasaw Indians, 8, 9, 11
cities, *5*, 6. *See also specific cities*
civil rights, 13, 15, 36
Civil War, 4, 12, *13*, 14, 36
Clarksville, Tennessee, 6
climate, 4, 21
Clingmans Dome, 20
coal mining, 24, *26–27*
colleges, 18–19
constitution, 7, 28
Cosby Ramp Festival, 44
country music, 32, 33
Country Music Hall of Fame and Museum, 7, *34*
courts, 30
Cove Lake State Park, 34–35
crafts, 32
Creek Indians, 8, 9
Crockett, Davy, 4, 10
culture and lifestyle, 27, 32–37
Cumberland Gap, 9
Cumberland Gap National Historical Park, 7
Cumberland Mountain State Park, 35
Cumberland Plateau, 20, 35
Cumberland River, 21, 22, 23
Cumberland Science Museum, *19*

D

dams, 14–15, 22, 26, 30
Darrow, Clarence, *14*, 19
De Soto, Hernando, 8
Democratic party, 30
Devil's Race Trace, 35
Doe River, *20*
Dogwood Arts Festival, 44
Duncan, John, Sr., 22

E

earthquakes, 22
East Tennessee, 18, 20, *20*, 21, 33
economy and commerce
    agriculture, 4, 11–12, 21, 25
    auto industry, 27
    chemical industry, 24

    coal mining, 24, *26–27*
    employers, 24
    fur trade, 8, 24
    furniture, 35
    Great Depression, 14–15, 26
    gross state product, *25*
    hydroelectric power, 26–27
    natural resources, 24–25
    New Deal, 14–15, 26, 35
    post-Civil War industries, 13–14
    Tennessee Valley Authority (TVA), *14–15*, 22, 26–27
    tourism, 15
    transportation, 13–14
education, 14, 18–19
electricity, 26–27
Elvis Week, 44
employers, 24
Endangered Species Act, 22
environmental issues, 22
epidemics, 13
Eskind Biomedical Library, 19
ethnic makeup of Tennessee, 16–18
European exploration, 8–9
events, 7, 32, 44–45
evolution, 14, *14*
executive branch, 28–29
exploration, 4, 8–9

F

Fan Fair, 44
Federal Express, 24
festivals, 32, 44–45
fish, 6, 22
Fisk University, 19, 35, *36*
flowers, 6, 23
foods of Tennessee, 7, 45
football, 37
forests, 23, 34
Forrest, Nathan Bedford, 14
Fort, Cornelia, 39
Fort Nashborough, 10
France, 8, 9
Franklin, Benjamin, 10
French and Indian War, 9
fur trade, 8, 24
furniture, 35

G

General Assembly, 28, 29, 30
geography, 4, 20–23
Giovanni, Nikki, 4, 38, 41
Gist, George (Sequoyah), 11
Gore, Albert, Jr., 41
Graceland, 15, 34
Grand Ole Opry, 7, *33*, 33, 34
Grant, Ulysses S., 12
Great Britain, 8, 9

Great Depression, 14, 26
Great Smoky Mountains National Park, *4–5*, 15, *23*, 23, 27, 34
Greeneville College, 19
gross state product, *25*
Gulf Coastal Plain, 21

H

Haley, Alex, 32, 36, 39, 40
Handy, W. C., 32, 33
Henderson, Richard, 9, 10
Hermitage, 37
Highland Rim, 21
highways, *5*
historic sites, 35–36
history of Tennessee, 8–15, *42–43*
hockey, 37
hogs, 23
Hood, John Bell, 12
Hooks, Benjamin, 15
horses, 6, 25, 45
house of representatives, 28
Houston Museum of Decorative Arts, 35
Hughes, Thomas, 35
Hull, Cordell, 29
Hunter Museum of American Art, 35
hydroelectric power, 26–27

I

immigration, 16–18
Indian Removal Act, 11
insects (state), 6
interstate highways, *5*

J

Jackson, Andrew, *10*, 11, *31*, 31, 37
James White's Fort, *9*
jazz music, 33
Jean and Alexander Heard Library, 19
Johnson, Andrew, 12–13, *31*, 31
Johnson City, Tennessee, 18
Johnston, Albert Sidney, 12
Jolliet, Louis, 8
Jubilee Hall, *36*
judicial branch, 30
July 4th Celebration and Anvil Shoot, 45

K

Kentucky Lake, 21, 22
King, B. B., 32
King, Martin Luther, Jr., 15
Kingsport, Tennessee, 18
Knoxville, Tennessee, 6, *9*, 11, 18, 20, 24
Ku Klux Klan, 14

L

La Salle, René-Robert Cavelier de, 8
Lake Barkley, 21
lakes, *5*, 21, *22*
legislative branch, 28, 29
Lenoir City, Tennessee, 22
libraries, 19, 36
Lincoln, Abraham, 12
literature, 4, 32, 36, 39–40, 41
Lookout Mountain, 12, *35*
Lost Sea, 7
Lynn, Loretta, 32

M

Manhattan Project, 15
maps of Tennessee, *5, 22, 25*
Marquette, Jacques, 8
McKissack and McKissack, 7
Memphis, Tennessee, 6, 7, 8, 21, 24, 33
Memphis Grizzlies, 37
Memphis in May International Festival, 45
Memphis International Airport, 27
Middle Tennessee, 17, 20, 21
Mississippi River, 9, 21, 22, 23
"Monkey Trial." *See* Scopes Trial
motto (state), 6
Mound Builders, 8
Mountain Farm Museum, 34
Mule Day, 45
museums, 7, 34–36
music, 4, 7, 27, 32–34, 40–41, 44–45

N

Nashville, Tennessee, 6, 10, 11, *18*, 21, 24, 33
Nashville Basin, 17, 21
Nashville International Airport, 27
Nashville Predators, 37
National Civil Rights Museum, 36
National Cornbread Festival, 45
National Storytelling Festival, 32, *45*
Native Americans, 4, 8–9, 11
natural resources, 24–25
Needham, James, 8
New Deal, 14–15, 26, 35
New Madrid earthquake, 22
newspapers, 36–37
Nineteenth Amendment, 30

O

Oak Ridge, Tennessee, 15, 26
Opryland, 34

outdoor recreation, 34–35
Overmountain Men, 10

P

parks, *4–5*, 7, *23*, 27, 34–35, 44
Parton, Dolly, 4, 16, 41
party politics, 30
Peabody Hotel, 7
Pearl, Minnie, 38–39
Perkins, Carl, 32
Phillips, Sam, 32, 40
Pioneer Farmstead, *4–5*
plants, 4, *21*, 23
politics and political figures
   Attakullakulla (Cherokee leader), 9
   Baker, Howard, 22
   Blount, William, 8, 10
   Bryan, William Jennings, 14
   Crockett, Davy, 4, 10
   Duncan, John, Sr., 22
   executive branch, 28–29
   Franklin, Benjamin, 10
   General Assembly, 29, 30
   Gore, Albert, Jr., 41
   Grant, Ulysses S., 12
   Hooks, Benjamin, 15
   Hull, Cordell, 29
   Jackson, Andrew, *10*, 11, *31*, 31, 37
   Johnson, Andrew, 12–13, *31*, 31
   judicial branch, 30
   King, Martin Luther, Jr., 15
   legislative branch, 29
   Lincoln, Abraham, 12
   party politics, 30
   Polk, James K., *31,* 31
   Roosevelt, Franklin Delano, 14, 26
   self-government, 9
   Sequoyah (George Gist), 11, *11*
   Sevier, John, 10–11, 38
   Willis, A. W., Jr., 15
Polk, James K., *31,* 31
Polk, Sarah Childress, 28
population, 6, 10, 14, 16–19
Presley, Elvis, 4, 32, *32,* 33–34, 40, 44
publishing, 36–37
Pulaski, Tennessee, 14

R

racial makeup of Tennessee, 16–18
racism, 14, 15
railroads, 13
rainfall, 21
Reconstruction, 12–13

recreation, 34–35
Reelfoot Lake, 22
religion, *17*, 19
Republican party, 30
Revolutionary War, 10
rivers, *5*, 21, *22*, 23, 26–27
roads, *5*
Roan Mountain State Park, 35
rock and roll, 33–34
Roosevelt, Franklin Delano, 14, 26
Roots (Haley), 36, 40
Rudolph, Wilma, 40–41
Rugby, Tennessee, 35

S

schools, 18–19
Scopes, John, 14
Scopes Trial, *14*
Scopes Trial Play & Festival, 45
seal of Tennessee, *28*
segregation, 15
senate, 28
Sequoyah (George Gist), 11, *11*
settlers, 4, 9–10, 16
Sevier, John, 10–11, 38, *38*
Shiloh National Military Park, 36, 44
slavery, 9, 11–12
Smithville Fiddlers' Jamboree and Crafts Festival, 45
Smoky Mountains, 20, *21*
snowfall, 9, 21
songs (state), 6
sports, 37, *37*, 40–41
Standard Candy Company, 7
statehood, 6, 10–11
steamships, 12
Stokes, Frank Wilbert, 36
Stones River National Battlefield, 36
Sun Studios, 32
Supreme Court (U.S.), 11, 22

T

Taylor, Peter, 32
Tellico Dam, 22
temperature, 21
Tennessee River, 20, 21, 22, 23, *42–43*
Tennessee State Museum, 35
Tennessee State University, 19
Tennessee Titans, 37
Tennessee Valley Authority (TVA), 14–15, *15*, 22, 26–27
Tennessee Walking Horse, 25
Tennessee Walking Horse National Celebration, 45
time line of Tennessee history, *42–43*

Tom Brown's School Days (Hughes), *35*
tourism, 15
Trail of Tears, 11
transportation, 13–14
Transylvania Purchase, 10
trees, 6, 23, 27
Tribute to Martin Luther King, Jr., 45
Tusculum College, 19

U

University of Tennessee, 18, 37
University of the South, 19
urbanization, 17
U.S. Department of Energy, 27
U.S. Supreme Court, 11, 22

V

Vanderbilt University, 19
Vaughn, Margaret Britton, 24
voting, 13, 30

W

War of 1812, 8, *10*, 11
Warren, Robert Penn, 32
waterways, *5*
Watts Bar Lake, 21
Wautauga Association, 7, 9
Wautauga River, 9
weather, 4, 21
West Tennessee, 17, 20, 21, 22, 33
West Tennessee Strawberry Festival, 45
Wilderness Trail, 9
wildlife, 4, 6, 7, *20*, 23–24
Willis, A. W., Jr., 15
World War II, 15, 26–27
World's Fair, 15

Y

yellow fever, 13